Mike's Guide
To Better Slot Play

M. J. Veaudry

ISBN - 13: 978-1450518055
ISBN - 10: 1450518052

High Praise for
Mike's Guide to Better Slot Play

"Like most slot players, I started playing slots just for the entertainment value. The bells and whistles were a welcome relief from the workweek and there was always the allure of a big payout. The more I played, the more intrigued I became by the workings of the slot machines. And as losing nights at the casino happened more than winning nights, I started to believe there must be a system, a strategy, to beat the machines.

I read every slot strategy book at the local library and even ordered a couple of titles online. The advice was usually the same; play quarter or dollar reel slots instead of penny video slots and always play maximum credits. I took the advice. Occasionally I'd get a nice payout, but more often than not, I'd go home with less than I started with, or nothing. I resigned to the fact the house advantage on the slots was too much and there was no way to win.

When I stumbled onto Mike's Guide to Better Slot Play, I was immediately intrigued because the author advocated playing penny video slots with less than maximum credits but with higher multipliers. This advice ran against everything I'd read before. I took the plunge and bought the book.

In the book, I found a simple way to "test" the looseness of a machine before I put all my money into it. I found a simple style of play, not a strategy really, to play with less money but at least cover my bet when hitting a winning combination. Finally, I found a method of betting that lowered my bet when I lost but increased my bet when I won, increasing my chances of hitting a winning combination when betting higher.

My first night at the casino, using the suggestions in Mike's Guide to Better Slot Play, I started with $250.00 and left with almost $350.00. I had several nice payouts of $20.00 to $90.00 and even on the machines that I didn't win a lot of money on I left just a dollar or two shorter than I started with. It was the first night I've had at the casino, in a long time, when I didn't feel the stress of trying to play to catch up to what I lost.

Forget the secrets, strategies, and systems. For an honest look on the history of slots, how slots work, and simple, straightforward, and effective suggestions on playing slots, this book is a must read!"

E.W. Omaha, NE

Dedication

This book is dedicated to anyone who likes to play slot machines and is interested in extending their play without spending more money to do so.

The process, rules and techniques outlined in this book can help you, regardless of your level of play. Whether you play the minimum bet or the maximum bet the book can help you play longer and go home with money in your pocket.

I sincerely hope you enjoy reading Mike's Guide to Better Slot Play. If you do, you may want to purchase Mike's Guide to Las Vegas, also available in paperback on Amazon or in electronic form on Kindle.

If you have any questions, comments or suggestions, you can always reach me at my Author's Page on Amazon.

Mike

CONTENTS

1.0 Introduction

I have been playing slot machines for over 25 years. Like most people I didn't need any instruction – just put your money in and pull the handle. As the years went by the SPIN button replaced the handle but the game was basically the same. Friends and relatives always told me to "bet the max" so I did. In fact, when I told a good friend of mine that I was writing this book he said: "well there can't be much to say – just bet the max". I told him he would have to read the book when it was finished.

It was only after many years of losing my money that I decided to find out more about slots – how they worked and strategies that would increase my winnings and extend my playtime.

I am not saying that if you follow my advice you will be a big slot winner. Winning a BIG JACKPOT relies entirely on luck. But you will play longer for the same amount of money and you will get more enjoyment out of the game if you follow my advice. After all, playing slots, like all other forms of gambling is entertainment. If it is not entertainment for you, then you might need professional help. But, if like most of us, you are playing for entertainment then the advice you will get in *Mike's Guide to Better Slot Play* should significantly increase your entertainment value and you may actually go home with money. No one likes to go home broke.

The first thing I want to tell you is *Mike's Golden Rule*: Before you go to the casino there are three things you must do:

1. Bring the cash with you that you have allotted for the entertainment – never bring more than you can afford to lose.

2. Decide how long you will stay – this is very important because far too often people start to play and if they win, they stay too long and lose it all or they chase their losses and end up losing even more.

3. Never bring a credit card or a bankcard into the casino. Leave these in your car or at home.

And most of all remember <u>it is time to leave</u> when you run out of money or you run out of time. If you have the <u>discipline</u> to do this you will get a lot more enjoyment out of your trips to the casino.

I realize that not everyone can leave when they want to, they are with other people or they have to wait for transportation, so if you are in this situation – bring a book or something else to amuse you. When I'm out of money and my wife or friends are still playing I will go to the lounge and have a drink, watch the game on the big screen, read the book I always carry with me for these occasions or just watch the people.

I cannot emphasize enough that if you do not want to be a victim of gambling then you really do need to develop discipline. In fact, discipline and patience are probably the most important attributes of a good slot player.

So let's get started with a Brief History of the Slot Machine so you know what you're up against.

2.0 A Brief History of the Slot Machine

I have a particular interest in the history of things and how they work, so much of what I cover in this book will deal with these two subjects because they interest me and I hope will interest you.

Gambling is one of the oldest known pursuits of humans. It has been in existence from the very earliest cave dwellers. Dice-like objects made from the anklebones of sheep or dogs have been found dating back 40,000 years. Gambling is indeed in our bones.

While it is impossible to pinpoint who actually developed a particular game, whether it was of Chinese, Greek, Roman or other origin one thing everyone can agree on is who invented the first mechanical slot machine.

Even though there were other slot machines in use at the time – called "nickel in the slot" machines that copied simple table games. The most of these was a poker machine that dealt out poker hands with no chance of a draw. You never won much but because of the popularity of poker these machines were also popular.

It wasn't until the creation of a unique game with a better payout that these machines really took off. For this we need to thank a young mechanic from San Francisco.

2.1 The Mechanical Slot Machine

Charles Fey, a 25-year-old mechanic, invented the first mechanical slot machine (the Liberty Bell) in San Francisco in 1887.

The picture below is of a typical saloon with the Liberty Bell slot machine bolted to the bar.

The following clip ran in the San Francisco Chronicle on April 15th, 1887:

"A group of owners of Saloons and Restaurants, of Market, Mission Enbarkadera and Barbary Coast gathered this morning in the small machine shop of Charles Fey at 631 Howard St. to view Mr. Fey's entirely new Liberty Bell, a machine featuring 3 reels mostly hidden with Horseshoes, Spades, Diamonds, Hearts, Bells symbols on reels. The device is operated by depositing a nickel in a slot to release the handle, when the right combination of symbols stop on the window the player is awarded coins ranging from 2, on 2 Horseshoes to 10 for 3 Bells. Most of those present agreed the machine should be a great success."

Local merchants immediately accepted the machine and Fey devoted most of his time to making these machines in his garage. He installed the machines with local merchants and received 50% of the profit made from the machines.

As the demand for Liberty Bell slot machines grew, Fey found it hard to meet the demand in his small shop. Gambling supply manufacturers tried to buy the manufacturing and distribution rights to the Liberty Bell but Fey refused to sell.

In 1907, Herbert Mills, a Chicago manufacturer of arcade games began production of a slot machine called the Operator Bell (a knock-off of Fey's Liberty Bell machine). Not surprisingly, the Operator Bell machine debuted just a few months after one of Fey's Liberty Bell machines went missing from a local saloon.

There were no patent laws on gaming equipment at the time.

By 1910 slot machines had found their way across the country. Mills and Company produced over 30,000 of these machines in just a few years.

While the demand for slot machines continued to grow rapidly, it didn't last. In 1909 slot machines became illegal in San Francisco and in Nevada a year later. By 1911 they were banned in California and by the 1930's it was politically popular to be anti-gambling and anti-slot machine. In spite of federal law prohibiting the inter-state transport of slot machines the number of illegal machines continued to grow. Today there are over 1 million slot machines installed in the country.

The original Liberty Bell machine was on display at the Liberty Belle Saloon and Restaurant in Reno, Nevada until it closed a few years ago.

2.2 Improvements to Stop Cheaters

Mechanical slot machines had a number of failings that made it easy for people with just a little knowledge to cheat the one-armed bandits. Some of the more colorful ways included:

Spooning a technique where the spooner would push the handle of a teaspoon into the coin return opening, to wedge open the little trapdoor, put a coin into the slot and pull the lever thereby receiving a payout on any combination. Manufacturers got wise to this idea and put two sharp angles on the pay chute making it impossible to insert anything up the chute.

Drilling was a technique used when slot machine cabinets were made of wood. The driller would use a special tool to drill a small hole through the cabinet directly opposite the payout slides. They would then insert a hooked wire, catch the bottom payout slide, pull it and receive a payout after each play. This didn't last too long before the manufacturers started lining the cabinet with drill-proof steel sheets.

The Rhythm System however was the most effective technique for emptying mechanical slot machines. In fact, it was so effective that the gaming industry shut down all slot machines in the country for three years (1948 – 1950) while they tried to figure out how to beat this technique.

This all started in 1948 when a "mysterious stranger" (yes, that's how the casino described him at the time) walked into the Golden Nugget on Fremont St. in Las Vegas and began playing a nickel slot machine. Within an hour he had hit jackpots on a number of machines and left town with over $500 (a good sum at that time). The casino bosses were left scratching their heads and hoping he would never return. But he did return and he brought friends with him. They would descend on a casino, empty a number of slot machines and disappear. But after a few visits the casinos were waiting for them and while they couldn't tell how they were doing it, they did manage to follow them when they left.

The mysterious man was an Idaho farmer who helped a friend repair mechanical slot machines in the winter months. He discovered that all slot machines were not random and that some of them had a clock fan that gave the player a 7-8 second window in which to determine the settings in the next pull. By learning the order of the symbols on the reels he was able to determine the rhythm needed to obtain a payout. By practicing, he determined how much pressure to put on the handle to get a particular result. However, now that the casinos knew who he was he started to get worried. Remember who controlled the casinos at this time.

The next time he went to Vegas he rented some office space and started offering classes on how to use the rhythm system to anyone who could pay the $5 fee. A lot of people took his classes and when they left the course and went into the casinos they put a big dent into slot machine revenues. In fact, in one year between 1948 and 1949 the national slot machine revenue dropped from $700 million to under $200 million. This would have been a great time to be a slot player. The casinos began banning anyone suspected of using the rhythm system and lawsuits were filed on both sides. But bit-by-bit casinos shut down their slot machines.

It took almost two years but by 1951 the slot manufacturers had developed and installed on each machine a device they called a "variator" that ensured that each play was completely random and independent from the previous play. The variator was a mechanical device that controlled the clock mechanism so that each spin starts at different times thereby making it impossible to use the rhythm system. Thus ended one of the most successful techniques to beat a mechanical slot machine.

2.3 EPROMs and Randon Number Generators

This is the technical section of the book. The place where I explain everything you ever wanted to know about how slot machines work. It probably contains a lot more information than most people would like to know but I find this stuff interesting and some of you may as well.

If you don't want to get this much information you can skip most of this section. Just go to the end of the section and read the summary I have included just for you (really - it's OK).

However, if you do want to know more let's start with the inventor of the EPROM.

Dev Froham, an Israeli engineer, invented the EPROM (Erasable Programmable Read Only Memory) chip in 1971. The EPROM (pictured below) was significant because it not only retained the data on it (in spite of power failures) but it was also easily programmable. Two characteristics that made it ideally suited to the modern slot machine.

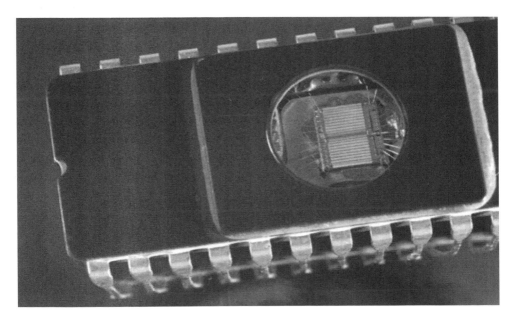

On May 15, 1984 Inge Telnaes, a theoretical Norwegian mathematician applied for patent # 4448419. The patent was for the "virtual stop". The concept allowed slot machines to get beyond the limited number of physical stops on a mechanical reel. By using a virtual reel, slot machines could offer much larger payouts and the mega jackpot was born.

All modern slot machines contain EPROMs. The EPROM is programmed by the manufacturer to deliver a particular payout percentage (for example 90.4%). However, casinos will order a number of machines with different payout percentages. The machines with the highest percentage payouts will be placed strategically in the casino to encourage the greatest action. While the lower payout machines will occupy the remaining spots.

The manufacturer also does the programming of the EPROM. The purpose of the programming is to map a random number to a virtual stop on a reel on the slot machine that can then be mapped to physical symbols in a specific location on that reel. This is where the Random Number Generator (RNG) comes in. The RNG generates a random number that is subsequently divided by a fixed number (the number of virtual stops) to produce a remainder (between 1 and N) that corresponds to the N possible combination of symbols pertaining to each stop on a virtual reel of a specific slot machine. Each stop on the virtual reel will contain the specific symbols that will appear in the slot machine display window. Not all symbols on the reel have the same probability of occurring. For example, a jackpot symbol usually occurs only once on a reel while there may be many occurrences of a lesser payout symbol on the same reel.

Once the random number is generated and the remainder is obtained, it is then mapped to a virtual stop on a reel to determine the corresponding symbols that will be displayed in the slot machine window.

This might be better understood with an example:

- Let's use a slot machine with 3 reels and 3 visible symbols per reel (one <u>above</u> the middle line, one <u>on</u> the middle line and one <u>below</u> the middle line).

- Suppose the EPROM chip's program, using the RNG returns the random number 10653942.

- Also suppose there are 6 unique possible symbols ($S_1 - S_6$) on a given reel, then there are 6 choose 3 possible combinations of these symbols or 20 {(6x5x4x3x2x1) / [(3x2x1) x (3x2x1)]} possible outcomes. This means that there are 20 virtual stops on each reel. This is a very simplistic example and no current slot machine would ever have such a small number of possible outcomes per reel. Nevertheless, by keeping the outcomes small it is easier to follow the example.

- However, to control the payout percentage for the slot machine we are going to add 12 more stops to bring the total number of stops to 32. Still too small for a modern slot machine but large enough for our example.

- The program divides the random number by 32 to determine the remainder: 22. In other words 32 x 332935 + 22 = 10653942. The program then looks at the 22nd virtual stop on the reel (from a table) to identify the 3 symbols (say S_a, S_b, S_c) that will be displayed on the first reel of the slot machine (one symbol S_a <u>above</u> the middle line, one symbol S_b <u>on</u> the middle line and one symbol S_c <u>below</u> the middle line).

- This process is repeated two more times until the symbols for all three reels are determined.

- The program then runs an algorithm to decide the payout by checking the alignment of all 6 symbols based on the number of lines played.

- Based on the 32 possible virtual stops on each reel, there are 32,768 (32x32x32) possible outcomes on any given spin. All of this takes place in a fraction of a second and is triggered as soon as you press the spin button or pull the handle.

Of course all reels on a given slot machine do not need to contain the same number of virtual stops. Some machines will have a wild or a scatter symbol that will only occur on certain reels. Other machines even when they have the same number of symbols on a reel might have fewer stops because some combinations of symbols might not be allowed on a reel. By adding and deleting stops on the reels (as we have done in our example) the manufacturer can control the probability of getting specific payouts. In this way the overall payout percentage is controlled <u>over the long run</u>.

The following table (using the example above for a $1 slot machine) describes this best.

Symbol	Pays	Reel 1	Reel 2	Reel 3	Occurrences	Payout
$3S_1$	$500	2	3	2	12	$6,000
$3S_2$	$150	3	3	4	36	$5,400
$3S_3$	$100	3	3	3	27	$2,700
$3S_4$	$50	5	5	5	125	$6,250
$3S_5$	$10	8	8	8	512	$5,120
$3S_6$	$5	11	10	10	1,100	$5,500
Total Win					1,812	$30,970
Total Bet						$32,768
Return						94.5%

Please note that this is a very simple example and although it does demonstrate how the modern slot machine works it is only an example and does not represent any particular machine.

While the explanation of how the EPROM and RNG work on a slot machine may be complex, there are a few important points you need to remember that can be used to improve your slot play:

1. The EPROM never gets reset and is running constantly and so is the RNG, generating thousands of random numbers every second.

    Consequently, never feel bad if you leave a machine and the next person sitting down gets a jackpot. The chances are very good that if you had stayed at that machine you would not have pressed the spin button at exactly the same instant that the next person did to win the jackpot. This also means that you do not need to flee the area just to avoid being there if that next person should happen to win a jackpot on a machine you were playing.

    I was playing at Caesar's Palace in Las Vegas years ago on a progressive machine in a carrousel. I was moving around the carrousel when a woman sat at the machine I had just played. On her first spin she won the jackpot - $1.4 million. All I could do was to congratulate her and step aside as the security men surrounded her.

2. The result of a particular spin is already determined before the reels stop spinning.

Consequently, don't be fooled into thinking that because you just missed a jackpot you can feel that there is one on the way. Every spin is random. You should also know that many of the virtual stops on the reel are designed to trigger a "near-miss". Usually a jackpot on a line you cannot play. Slot machine programs capitalize on the near-miss effect. Researchers have found that manufacturers program their games to tease players with near misses about 30% of the time (a number psychologists have found optimal for getting gamblers to keep playing).

3. The screen is an output device and only displays the results of a particular spin.

Consequently, even if the screen on a slot machine shows a jackpot, you will not be paid off unless the EPROM confirms that there is a jackpot. For smaller jackpots casinos usually just pay off based on what the screen shows, but if you win a large progressive jackpot don't be surprised if the casino moves everybody back from the machine while a technician opens the door and checks the EPROM to confirm that there really is a jackpot. If the EPROM shows any signs of tampering (deliberate or accidental) the casino will not pay out the jackpot regardless of what the screen shows. Read carefully the small print on every slot machine that says all results are void in the event of a malfunction. There are many lawsuits outstanding against casinos where players believe they should have won a jackpot but the casino refuses to pay them. In most cases these are ruled in the casino's favor.

Summary (for those who didn't read the detail)

The key things you need to know about modern slot machines:

1. All modern slot machines have a computer chip in them that is programmed with a random number generator that is constantly generating random numbers at thousands of times per second.

2. Slot machines are programmed to payout at a pre-determined percentage (set by the manufacturer - not the casino). Not all machines in a casino payout at the same percentage. This is why some machines are tight (lower percentage payout) and other machines are loose (higher percentage payout).

3. All results are determined as soon as the spin button is pushed or the handle pulled.

4. The spinning of the reels has nothing whatsoever to do with the result. The spinning of the reel is only there for entertainment value.

5. The slot machine manufacturers put in the spinning reels to add more excitement for the player   most people wouldn't find it very interesting or exciting if they pushed the spin button and immediately the result was displayed. This would certainly speed up the play and make more money for the casino but a lot of people wouldn't want to play if this was the case.

6. The screen on the slot machine is just an output device. Its only purpose is to communicate the result to the player - a result that has already been determined before the reels even start to spin.

2.4 The Modern Slot Machine

Most people play Slots – sad but true. Over 70% of casino revenues come from slot machines. Most people who play these machines also have no idea what they are doing. The popularity of slot machines is that you don't need to know anything to play them; all you need is that one spin that will pay you a jackpot to be a winner. You would be amazed at the number of people who can't wait to put their money into a machine without any idea of what it takes to win or what makes a good bet. I've lost count of the number of people I've met who only know two things – bet the max and hit the spin button as fast as possible. This is a great strategy for the casino but a very bad strategy for the slot player.

2.5 Types of Slot Machines

There are four basic types of slot machines in use today; the modern Mechanical slot machine, the Video slot machine, the REEL slot machine and the Progressive slot machine. Each type is exactly the same internally (insomuch as each machine has an EPROM chip and is programmed with a Random Number Generator to generate a predictable payout percentage).

On the outside however, they are very different. One has a mechanical drum that has a fixed number of stops and the others are video slot machines with an indeterminate number of virtual stops. Some are progressive machines that offer a mega jackpot while others offer medium size payouts.

Each type of slot machine requires a slightly different technique of play and different betting strategy. On some like the progressive machines you must play the maximum bet while on others like the video slot machine you would be ill advised to play the maximum bet.

Let's look at each of these types of machines in turn to get a better understanding of how they work and what strategies will work best on each particular type of machine.

The Modern Mechanical Slot Machine

The modern Mechanical slot machine, pictured above, usually has 1, 3 or 5 pay lines. The machine usually has three mechanical drums or reels that are spun independently and stopped on a pay line to show the outcome of the spin. The EPROM chip controls these machines and a random number generator (RNG) like those described in section *2.3 EPROMS and Random Number Generators* determines where to stop each reel.

The major difference between these machines from those described below is that the drum has a physical limitation and therefore the number of stops on the drum is also limited. Consequently, the probability of winning on a given spin is easier to determine – $1/n^3$ (where n is the number of symbols on each of the 3 reels). Generally the probability of winning on a modern Mechanical slot machine is better than on a Video slot machine that has an indeterminate number of virtual stops.

Another difference between these machines and Video slot machines is that the casino can weight the stops and thereby affect the outcomes and the percentage payouts. On a video slot machine with virtual stops the casino has no way of making adjustments since the manufacturers' programming controls all results.

The down side to these machines is that they do not provide the same level of excitement that Video slot machines deliver through bonus games and extra features. They are usually higher denomination machines: typically $0.25 and up. There was a time, not that long ago, when these machines dominated the casino floor. This is not the case today.

The Video Slot Machine

DAVINCI DIAMONDS (pictured above) is an example of a Video slot machine. The video slot machine became very popular in the 80's. Invented by Walt Fraley in the mid-70's it was not widely played at first because people didn't trust these machines, after all, they didn't have mechanical drums that actually spun. This all changed however when video poker became popular.

The important thing to remember about Video slot machines is that they can have a lot more virtual stops (usually between 32 and 512) than the Mechanical slot machines that were restricted by the number of symbols you could get on the actual drum. This typically means that payouts are bigger on a Video slot machine than on Mechanical slot machines but the number of favorable outcomes (where you might actually get a win) can be a lot lower on the Video slot machine than on a Mechanical slot machine.

Video slot machines also allowed manufacturers much more flexibility in designing their games. Many of these machines have bonus games or additional spins. The DAVINCI DIAMONDS machine above offers tumbling reels where the symbols making up a win will evaporate after the payout and drop down allowing new symbols to enter the screen. In this way you can get multiple wins on a single spin.

Video slot machines also allowed the manufacturers to introduce multi-line machines. Previously, slot players could only alter their bets by increasing the number of credits played. By increasing the number of lines as well as the number of credits bet it was now possible to significantly increase the amount bet per spin. Many machines allowed 200 or 300 credits to be played per spin. Consequently the denomination you could bet was lowered. Since few people would bet 200+ quarters or higher on a Video slot machine the manufacturers reduced the denomination on these machines to nickels and eventually pennies.

When Video slot machines were first introduced it was hard to find a penny machine in a casino but now the 1 and 2 cent machines usually outnumber all of the others. Today, most slot machines in a casino are Video slots.

The REEL Slot Machine

The popular CHOY SUN DOA machine pictured above is a good example of a REEL machine. Look for a symbol on the side of the screen that says <u>REEL POWER</u> or <u>243 WAYS TO WIN</u>.

It represents a class of machines where you bet the number of reels and not the number of lines. A payout is made regardless of where the symbols appear on the reel, since there are no fixed lines per se. The middle row on each reel is free and is always in play regardless of the number of reels played.

The REEL machine is my favorite because you do not need to decide how many lines to play only the number of reels (1 – 5) you want to play starting from left to right. A symbol will play regardless of where it is on a reel as long as there are consecutive symbols. This means that if you play:

- 1 reel there is 3 (3x1x1x1x1) ways to win (since the middle row is free regardless of the number of reels you play). In other words all of the symbols on reel 1 will be in play and the middle symbols on reels 2 – 5. To have a win you will need the same symbol in the middle of reel 2 and 3 and it will need to be the same as one of the three symbols on reel 1;

- 2 reels there are 9 (3x3x1x1x1) ways to win,

- 3 reels there are 27 (3x3x3x1x1) ways to win,

- 4 reels there are 81 (3x3x3x3x1) ways to win and

- 5 reels there are 243 (3x3x3x3x3) ways to win.

The Progressive Slot Machine

Progressive slot machines (like those above) have become very popular and in cities like Las Vegas they offer exceptionally huge jackpots. In March 2003 a 25-year old software engineer from Los Angeles (who wanted to remain nameless) won a $38.7 million dollar jackpot at the Excalibur in Las Vegas. By linking machines together across a casino, city or state, Progressive jackpots can be enormous.

The most important thing to remember about Progressive slot machines is that the payouts other than the jackpot are not as good as on other machines because a portion of every bet made goes towards the jackpot. Many of the new progressives are like the one above where there are smaller jackpots unique to the machine or a carousel of machines but where many will share the top jackpot prize. If the jackpot is very large it can be shared among numerous casinos, within a local area or across a state. Needless to say, these jackpots can get very large.

The other thing to remember is that to win a progressive jackpot you need to bet the maximum number of credits. To bet fewer than the maximum on these machines would be foolish because as I have already said the payout is not as good as other machines and even if you get a payout the amount will be less than you would have gotten on a non-progressive machine of the same kind. Not to mention the fact that it is very annoying when you want to play a Progressive machine only to discover that there are no machines available although there is that one person playing a single multiplier with no chance to win the jackpot. Go figure.

I make it a rule to only play Progressive machines if I am up money. I do not like to play these machines with my own money. I also will play for a very short time unless I actually win something. You can lose your money very quickly playing Progressive machines.

2.6 The Most Important Things to Remember

Now that we have had a chance to look at slot machines in detail, there are a number of things you need to remember.

1. All modern slot machines are controlled by a computer chip with a random number generator that is generating random numbers at thousands of times per second (even when the machine is not being played).

2. When you interrupt the machine by pressing the spin button or pulling the handle a result is immediately determined based on the random number generated at that instant you interrupted the machine.

3. The result of that interruption is shown to you by the symbols on the screen (the machine's output device). The spinning of the reels has nothing to do with the result that has already been determined. The spinning of the reels is just done to make the total experience more exciting.

4. In setting up the virtual stops on the reels the manufacturer has created a number of "near misses" (about 30% of the results are near misses) to encourage you to bet more lines, play longer or even increase the multiplier you are betting.

5. Modern Mechanical slot machines (usually denominations of 25 cents and higher) offer the best payouts, followed by REEL Machines that are a better price performer than Video slot machines. The lowest payouts are from Progressive slot machines.

3.0 Myths About Playing Slot Machines

1. Always make the maximum bet – NOT TRUE.

This is the quickest way to lose your money. The payout is not determined by the amount bet but by the multiplier (x) bet regardless of the number of lines played. For example, assume you are playing a 5-cent machine with 9 lines and multipliers from 1 – 5. The maximum bet would cost you 45 nickels ($2.25). Suppose the jackpot paid out $500. In this case you are winning the jackpot because you played the 5-line multiplier not because you played 9 lines. If you played nine lines but only played a 1x multiplier (I see a lot of people do this) you would only win $100 on the same payout. However, if you only played 1 line with a 5x multiplier you might still have won the $500 jackpot but you would only have played 5 nickels (25 cents). The important point to remember is that the multiplier has a bigger impact on the outcome than the number of lines played.

You can continue to bet the maximum and lose your money quickly while waiting for a jackpot or you can bet fewer lines but still bet the maximum multiplier (x) and play a lot longer. In this particular example, I would prefer to play 5 lines at a 5x multiplier (for a total cost of $1.25). Consequently I would get 180 spins compared to the 100 spins a person would get playing the maximum bet.

So stop playing the maximum number of lines and start playing the maximum multiplier.

2. I've just won a jackpot so I should leave the machine, it won't pay again – NOT TRUE.

The very best machines you can play are those where the person has taken their win and left leaving the winning combination on the screen. A lot of people see this and won't sit down but don't be fooled. Machines that have just paid out might be looser machines than a machine that has not been paying. If you had a choice – would you play a loose machine or a tight machine? I know the one I would pick.

I wouldn't put a lot of money in the machine but I would try 10 pulls to see if it is still active. I've lost count on the number of times I have played these machines and won. There is actually a mathematical theorem that shows that even in a system of numbers generated randomly there can be repeated patterns. In other words there can be a cluster of winning combinations even in a random sample of spins. So don't be too quick to leave your winning machine.

3. I've been so close to the jackpot. If I play a little longer I know I'll win – NOT TRUE.

Remember, slot machines have a random number generator in them so there is a random factor and as such there is no predictability of any outcome. Also, the people who program these machines want to keep you playing so they often show results that are close to a jackpot, these are called near misses. So if you see a jackpot on a line you are not playing don't be fooled. If the program determines that a jackpot should be paid you would have got it on one of the lines you were playing. Putting the jackpot on a line you are not playing also has the extra affect of getting you to play more lines and consequently bet more money.

4. I left a machine and the next person got a jackpot, I shouldn't have left – NOT TRUE.

Slot machines today have a built in random number generator (RNG) that is continuously cycling through thousands of numbers a second. When you press the spin key or pull the handle the RNG selects a number that determines the outcome and the symbols on the reels. This is all done in a split-second and it is extremely likely that if you had stayed at that machine you would not have had the same outcome as the next person.

5. The casino is tightening its slots; no one is winning anything – NOT TRUE.

It is impossible for casinos to alter the payout percentages on Video slot machines. These machines are purchased from the manufacturer with set payout percentages. The EPROM chip the manufacturer puts into

26

the machine determines the payout percentage. These chips are sealed and cannot be tampered with. Although, modern Mechanical slot machines do have drums in them and the casino could weight the stops to affect the percentage payout there are relatively few of these machines in most casinos and they are often lightly played so it is unusual for the casino to tamper with these machines.

6. The machines at the entrance and end of aisles pay off more often – NOT TRUE.

This is not the case anymore. When everyone discovered this secret the smart casino managers moved the looser machines to other locations. The tighter machines have moved into these locations so don't play machines at the entrance or machines at the end of aisles.

The best locations for loose slots now are in locations that can be seen from anywhere in the casino (preferably raised areas that are easy to see). You will also find them near cafés and coffee shops since this is a way to get people to eat quicker and get back to the machines, particularly when they can hear them paying off while they are eating. You may also find them near redemption centers, change booths or ATM stations since the people waiting in line there are likely to change more cash or make larger withdrawals when they hear people winning more often. Another frequent location for loose slots is in crossover areas. Crossover areas are where players must walk through to get to other slot aisles. The casinos want slot players to witness frequent jackpot payouts. People passing by using these pathways are more likely to be drawn into the main slot aisles, where the medium and tight machines are waiting to fleece them.

4.0 Bankroll Management

How you manage your money depends a lot on how long your playing session will last. If you are going to the casino for the evening you need to manage your money differently than when you are going to Las Vegas for a week.

4.1 An Evening at the Casino

The most important thing for you to do if you are going to the casino for an evening (or maybe an afternoon or any short period of time) is to decide before you go how much you will put at risk (always something you can afford) and equally important how long you will stay.

Almost everyone will take cash with them to the casino but very few people set a time limit on how long they will play. The time limit is even more important than the amount of money you take with you because it determines when you will leave and if you will take money home with you. In other words, whether you will be a winner or a loser. People who leave when they run out of time will almost always take money home with them.

Most sensible people will leave before they run out of money but if you stay long enough, YOU WILL LOSE ALL OF YOUR MONEY. Just think of the number of times this has happened to you. Then think about how things could have been different if you had just left earlier while you still had money in your pocket. It took me a long time to realize that it is always better to leave with money than to go home broke and feeling very bad.

If you are going with other people see if you can get all of them to agree on a time to leave.

When you lose your money you have to stop playing. The very worst thing you can do is to get more money. One of the basic rules I have that should never be broken is to leave your bankcard and credit cards at home.

It is too easy in the casino to go to the bank machine so leave these cards in your car or at home.

If you run out of money before the people you are with you can watch them play (very boring) or you can sit in the bar, have a drink or watch the game on the big screen. But do something that will get you out of the gaming area.

Bankroll Management is also about knowing how to save some of your winnings. I have a simple rule for this: whenever you win more money at a machine than you put into it always take the winnings and put them into a different pocket than the one containing your play money. I call this my **Going Home Pocket Rule**. Never spend the money in this pocket. It is your going home pocket. Never chase your losses. Once you lose the money you brought with you to play you are done playing.

This is probably the most difficult thing you will have to do. Believe me it is very tempting to dip into your Going Home Pocket when you are out of money to play with. A lot of my friends tell me that they were up money and could have left with money in their pocket but decided to play with it anyway because they were just there for an evening out. OK if you do this once in a while don't be too hard on yourself but if you are going to the casino regularly this is not a good habit to get into.

I can guarantee you that you are going home with no money in your pocket if you dip into your Going Home Pocket.

4.2 A Trip to a Gambling Destination

When you travel for a longer gambling session, say to Las Vegas or Atlantic City, you need to manage your money a little differently.

Unless you have an unlimited supply of money you are probably like the rest of us and have a limit on the amount you can spend on your slot entertainment.

Some lessons are hard to learn and some mistakes get repeated too often. It took me too long to realize that I had to do something better than just playing with increasingly larger amounts of money in an effort to have something to show for it. It seemed like no matter how much I took with me, it always found a way to disappear.

The wake up call for me came on one trip when I went with a group of guys and found I was out of money on the third day of a five-day visit. Oh yes, I know what you're thinking: "just go to a bank machine and get more cash" – right - wrong. Well, in those days they didn't have ABMs on every corner. You had to go to a bank to get cash and there weren't any banks near the casinos. Early on I made myself a promise that I would only spend what I took with me. However, I didn't promise anything about not borrowing a few bucks from my friends. After a modest stake from a good friend, I was very lucky to get a great run at the Black Jack table and made enough to pay back the stake and finish out the trip. But the lesson was learned and as a result of this experience I made some changes.

If you follow these few simple rules I can promise (well almost promise) that you will bring money back with you. This does not mean that you will necessarily bring back more money than you took with you, but whenever you bring money back, you always feel like a winner. Just follow these simple steps:

1. Before you leave home decide how much money (your **Bankroll**) you want to spend on gambling. I assume you will use a charge card for meals, accommodation, car rentals, shopping and other tourist activities. Since the casinos only deal in cash, determine before you go, how much money you are <u>willing and able</u> to lose before you leave home. It is never a good idea to take more money than you can afford to lose.

2. Once you determine the size of your bankroll, **break it down** into the number of **sessions** you plan to gamble. I like to separate the day into the morning, afternoon and evening sessions, with a different **stake** for each of these. Since I don't do much gambling in the morning this is always my smallest stake. The afternoon is a little more active for me so it is larger than the morning but smaller than the evening when I do most of my gambling. Although I use three sessions a day and a different stake for each, you may decide to limit yourself to one session for the entire day.

Just remember, the fewer the sessions you plan for, the harder it will be to manage your money.

3. Once you have broken down your bankroll into sessions the difficult part starts. Each session must have a specific start and end time. In my case, since I break my bankroll down into three sessions every day, the morning session starts when I wake up and ends at exactly 12:00 PM (noon). The afternoon session then starts and ends at exactly 6:00 PM. The evening session then begins and ends at a specific time. This may vary each day depending on how tired I am but there must be a defined time to stop gambling.

4. The discipline of establishing specific start and end times to each session (they don't have to be the same as the ones I use) is critical to the success of this approach to money management. At the start of each session we have just enough money for the session. The session is over when you run out of time or you run out of money – whichever comes first.

5. At the end of each session you must set aside whatever money you have left and this amount will be taken home. I usually keep the money I'm taking home in the room safe and in a separate place from the money that is set aside for gambling.

This technique requires a lot of discipline. Yes, I know it will be hard for you if your money runs out early in the session so you need to plan for this contingency. Experience has taught me that there will be more losing days than winning days, so be prepared to finish early on most of the days.

This is the time you go shopping, find the nearest bar, have a drink and watch the sports game, find a comfy chair and read your book, go back to the hotel and sit in the hot tub or just people watch. Whatever you do, get out of the gaming area. When you are losing you are most vulnerable, so unless you really want to throw good money after bad and end up feeling really stupid, walk away – no run away from the gaming area.

However, if you follow these rules you will be putting money away on your winning days and this will mean that you will be bringing money home with you. Believe me, nothing will make you feel better about a gambling holiday than bringing home money.

4.3 Basic Rules to Remember

1. Decide how much money you are going to take to the casino or on your trip before you go. Do not plan to get cash at the casino. Also take only money that you can afford to lose.

2. Decide in advance how long you are going to play. This is very important. When your time is up you must stop playing and leave the casino regardless of whether you are winning or losing. Whatever money you have is the money you are going home with.

3. If you start to win at a machine, set upper and lower limits for the remainder of your play at this machine. Never go below the lower limit and if you go above the higher limit set a new set of limits and continue to play the machine until you fall below the last lower limit at which time you should leave the machine. Don't walk away – run.

4. When you exceed a higher limit, cash out the ticket and take the money you have made in excess of what you started playing the machine with and physically put it in another pocket or in a different place in your purse. If you have a friend you can trust give it to them. I call this my **Going Home Pocket Rule**. The transfer of cash to this pocket is very important symbolically and psychologically because you are taking this money home with you regardless of how the remainder of your gambling session goes. This is the most discipline you will need during your session so do not falter or you will go home with nothing.

5. Always, always, always leave the casino when you are out of money, or you are out of time. If you are out of money and are waiting for others go to the car, sit in a comfortable chair, read a book, have a drink in the lounge (if you can pay for it), or just go out for a walk. But make sure you leave the gaming area immediately. This is the most important thing you will need to learn if you want to leave the casino with money. Most people leave the casino with no money. A lot of my friends tell me that they understand the Going Home Pocket Rule but they want to stay and play and they came to lose their money

in any case. I cannot help these people. So if you are one of these people and you just want to play until you lose all your money – good luck to you is all I can say.

5.0 Your Guide to Better Slot Play

Everyone knows how to play a slot machine. Most people just watch what others do and sit down and start to play. Some people might ask the person playing a similar machine – what to do. Or you may already have been told what to do by a friend or relative. In any event it usually doesn't take much knowledge to play a slot machine – right? Wrong. Most people do not have any idea about what is a good way or a bad way to play slot machines. They go to the casino with some money to lose, play until it is gone and leave.

I'm going to tell you a better way to play slots. What makes my technique a better way? It is all based on making your money last longer. Playing slot machines is entertainment and if I can show you some ways to stretch your entertainment dollars then its got to be a better way to play.

I've already said this but I will say it again. This book is not about winning a jackpot or making money playing slot machines. The truth is that there is no way to continually win money on slot machines. If someone tells you there is, they are lying or maybe just delusional.

This section of Mike's Guide to Better Slot Play will lead you through the basics of finding a machine to play, how to pick one machine over another, determining how much to bet, how long to play a losing machine and how to extend your play on a winning machine.

I sincerely hope that my advice will in some way make you a better slot machine player.

5.1 Finding a Machine to Play

How many of you know where the best slot machines are in a casino? At the entrance and on the ends of aisles – right – wrong. This was the case 20 years ago, but once everyone got to know this, the casino management decided it was time for a change. Something they have been doing ever since.

Remember, I mentioned earlier that casinos buy slot machines that are programmed for different payouts. Some have lower percentage payouts (tight machines) while others have higher percentage payouts (loose machines). The first thing you want to do when you enter a casino is to try and locate where these machines are.

One thing you can do is look where the locals are playing. You can often walk into a casino and find groups of machines that no one is playing – the tight machines. The locals know this by experience, there aren't as many people being paid off in these areas so they avoid them. DON'T PLAY HERE. Look for a loose machine in the crowded areas, even if you have to wait.

Speak with a slot machine attendant. They work here day-in and day-out and they know what machines are paying and what machines are not. If you are courteous and you look like you might give them a tip, should you win, they will be more than eager to help you locate one.

The other thing to remember is to start playing on machines that have moderate payouts. These are not machines that have progressive jackpots or even multi-level jackpots. The reason for this is simple; every progressive jackpot machine takes a portion of every play and puts this towards the jackpot. This means that Progressive machines payout a number of smaller prizes compared to their corresponding machines that are not progressive. They can get away with this because everyone is trying to win the one big prize and they are willing to overlook the lower payouts. The next time you are in a casino check out the payout for a Progressive Wheel of Fortune (for example a DOUBLE DIAMOND machine) and compare this payout to a non-progressive machine of the

36

same denomination and you will understand what I mean. Therefore, don't start out immediately playing Progressive machines. Play the standard machines until you can amass some winnings to use on the Progressive machines.

The other thing you can do is check out the following locations (areas where casino management are currently placing loose slots):

1. On elevated carousels. These don't have to be high limit slots just areas that can easily be seen from anywhere in the casino. Management knows that it is good for business when people see other people winning. So any area that is visible to a lot of people is a good area to put loose machines.

2. Near crossovers – areas where people have to walk to get to another area of the casino. These are an ideal place for management to place loose slots because they get a lot of traffic walking by.

3. Near cafes and snack bars – any place where people are not playing and can still see machines paying off. This is an incentive for them to eat quickly and get back to the machines.

4. Near change booths, cashiers, ABMs or redemption machines – places where people are getting money. The more they hear people winning the more likely they are to get more cash.

It is also important to know where the tightest slots are as these are places you do not want to play. They include:

1. Secluded areas where there are not many people. These areas may be quiet but they are quiet for a reason – no one is winning here.

2. The casino entrances used to be a great place for loose slots. But as people found out about this they never moved any further into the casino and management needed to make a change. In most casinos today, tight slots are at the entrance.

3. Near ticket/show lines – anywhere people are standing around and waiting. Many of these people will play the machines nearby rather than just wait in line. Often friends will take turns holding the other's place

while they venture out to play a machine. Do not play the machines closest to you. If a friend holds your place in line, go further into the casino to play.

4. Surrounding the table games. These machines are almost always tight. Since people who play table games are usually not regular slot players, these machines are there to take their money while they wait for a table.

5. Near the Sports Book. People playing the Sports Book almost always spend more money than slot players so casinos like to keep them in the Sports Book and having a loose slot paying off just outside the area is not a good idea.

6. If you go to Las Vegas to play, NEVER, NEVER, NEVER play the slots at the airport. They are the tightest slots in the state.

5.2 Reading the Slot Meter

Now that you have found an area to play slots in, which machine do you pick? Assuming you have picked a game that interests you and that there are several identical machines in the same area always pick the machine that has the highest amount in the payout meter window. This can usually be found in the bottom left or right hand corner of the machine next to the credit window. In the example above it is on the right marked WINNER PAID. This is the amount that the last player has cashed out of the machine. Yes, I know they may have started with more credits and the payout window shows the credits they left with. It does not mean that they won this amount. In fact, they could have lost a lot more than the amount showing.

You may also ask why this even matters since the machines are random and even if the last person won money this does not necessarily mean that the next person will win. You are right, of course, but the work of mathematician Gregory Chaitan proves that there are patterns even in systems of random numbers. If you have been playing slots a long time you will notice these patterns, short bursts when you get several wins at a time. It does not mean that the machine isn't random just that there are patterns even in systems of random numbers.

But, in the absence of any other information, would you rather play a machine that shows zero in the payout window or one like the one above that shows 320 credits. I know the one I always play. This is just a habit on my part but it does work more often than not.

I call this the **Pay & Pay Again (PPA) Rule**.

So always check the slot meter when you are walking around.

I particularly like to play a few pulls on a machine that has just paid off a jackpot like the one above. Call it superstition. But there are a lot of people who will leave a machine once they get a good win without even bothering to clear the payout window and try a few more credits. Look for these machines and play a few credits (I usually make five pulls) – you may be surprised at how many times you will win something using my PPA Rule.

5.3 Know the Game Rules

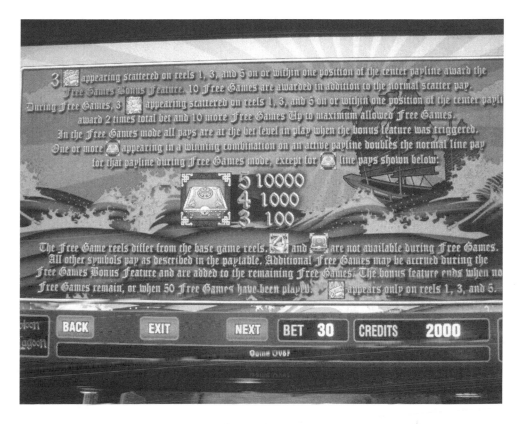

I can't tell you the number of times I have been playing a machine when the person beside me wins something and says: What did I do to win? Can you explain the game to me? If you have been in a similar situation you know how annoying this is. The worst case is when a person has won a bonus game or they are in the middle of a bonus game and the game is waiting for them to do something – like press the start feature button or make a selection on the screen. In any event they just sit wondering what to do. I usually explain it to them and then move on.

Do not play a game when you do not know the rules. Would you play Craps, Pai Gow Poker or any other casino game without first knowing the rules, then why would you play a slot machine without knowing the rules for the game?

I have a 3-point drill I follow when I sit down to play a slot machine.

1. Check the amount to play, depending on whether the machine is a single-line or multi-line machine.

Single line machines

I have already told you that if you sit down and just play the maximum number of credits your money will not last long. Therefore, take a few seconds to understand the payouts.

On a single line machine like the one above payouts are often printed at the top of the machine in columns displaying the amounts paid for one coin played, two coins played etc. These machines usually play a maximum of 5 coins. The one above is a 25-cent machine that takes a maximum of 3 credits (75 cents).

Most of these machines will offer you a bigger payout on the jackpot when you bet the maximum number of credits. In the example above all payouts are proportionate (3 red sevens pay 50 credits with one coin bet, 100 credits with 2 coins bet and 150 credits with 3 coins bet) except the highest payout where 3 multipliers (2x, 3x and 5x) will pay 1,000 credits when 1 coin is bet, 2,000 credits when 2 coins are bet but 4,000 credits when 3 coins are bet. The manufacturer does this to get you to play the maximum number of credits every time.

The other thing you need to watch for is when there are different payouts for different coins played. Some machines will only payout on certain combinations when you play a single coin, other combinations when you play two coins and still other combinations when you play a third coin. In other words if you get a winning combination that is paid when three coins are played and you only played one coin – you win nothing. This can be very disappointing. I was with a friend years ago in the Flamingo in Las Vegas who played a $1 coin in a machine just like the one I am describing. He got 3 flaming sevens on the pay line but didn't win anything because the 3 flaming sevens only paid off when you played 3 coins. Instead of winning $1000 he won nothing. He never made this mistake again. The lesson we should all learn from this is to carefully read the payouts before putting any coins into the machine.

On these single-line machines you only need to decide how many coins to play. I like machines where the maximum is only two coins. These are not expensive machines to play (compared to a lot of others) and they give you the chance to win a large prize (2,000 credits or $500 in this case) for a relatively small amount bet - $0.50.

This type of machine is usually a Mechanical slot machine. You may remember that these machines have a fixed drum with a specific number of symbols on each reel. Consequently, they have a better return because there are fewer stops. However, they can be very boring to play so they are not that popular in a casino.

I usually start my playing session on these machines. The denomination is up to you but I always like to start on a two-coin machine. After this I will move to a 3-coin and then a 5-coin machine. I like to play about 20% of by bankroll on these machines.

Multi-line Machines

On a multi-line machine like the one above carefully check the number of lines you can play. Pay particular attention to machines that offer a Bonus game <u>but only</u> if you play the maximum number of lines. This is the case with a class of machines called CASHMAN. The Bonus game only applies if you bet the maximum number of lines. I try to avoid these machines just because I do not like to bet the maximum number of lines. By doing so I usually have to reduce the multiplier bet to keep my total bet within my limits. I always like to play the maximum multiplier since this is where the money is, not in the number of lines played. I will say a lot more about this later.

A few years ago my wife was playing a CASHMAN machine and an elderly woman was sitting beside her. My wife was getting the CASHMAN bonus but the elderly woman was not. She wondered out loud why she was not getting the Bonus. My wife looked at the woman's machine and saw that she was playing 20 lines but not the maximum number of credits (25) to start the Bonus game. When my wife noticed this she told the woman that she could not get the Bonus unless she played 25 credits. The woman took her advice and within a few minutes got the Bonus game and won over $100 dollars. The woman did not understand how the game worked and because she normally played 20 lines, this is what she continued to do. So before you sit down to play a machine please take the time to understand how the game works and what you need to bet to get the payouts particular to the machine.

Some of the newer multi-line machines (like the one above) do not give you a choice of the number of lines played – they assume you will play the maximum number of lines. The machine above only lets you chose the multiplier – 1, 2, 3 or 4 times the number of lines. In this case you can bet 75, 150, 225 or 300 credits. In some ways this is similar to the REEL power machines that only give you a choice of the number of reels you can play (1 – 5). However, the payouts are not nearly as good. If possible, I will avoid machines like the one above. I would also urge you to do the same. If we don't play these machines (that are heavily weighted in the casinos favor) they will be replaced with something that is fairer for us, the slot player.

The bottom line is to pay careful attention to make sure you understand how many lines you can play and what limitations there might be on the number of lines.

Another example of how you need to be careful is the SEX AND THE CITY machine. This machine is a multi-game machine. You can play up to four simultaneous games. However, you cannot play a two or three times multiplier unless you play all four games simultaneously. Therefore it will cost 400 (50 x 4 x 2 = 400) credits to play a two times multiplier and 600 (50 x 4 x 3 = 600) credits to play a 3 times multiplier. This is a new type of machine – the multi-game machine. So be very sure you understand your line bet before you press the spin button.

I am very disappointed at the number of new machines I see coming into casinos across the country where the player has no choice in selecting the number of lines to play. The fewer choices the casino can give the player the less control the player has and the more money the casino will make. This will become obvious when we try to structure a betting strategy that will return more credits than the credits bet. If the lines you play are fixed at the maximum by the casino then the only way you can cover your bet is to play a larger multiplier and therefore a larger bet than you would have played otherwise. This will result in the casino earning even more from these machines. It is almost a certainty that we will see more of these machines unless people avoid playing them.

2. Check the Winner Paid Window.

As I said earlier if there are two machines the same I will always play the one with the higher WINNER PAID window.

The WINNER PAID window in the example above is in the top right corner of the screen. In this example the player won 320 credits. These windows can be anywhere on the machine. But every machine has one. Make a habit of looking for these windows before you decide which machine to play.

As I said earlier, given a choice, I will always play the machine with the highest WINNER PAID window.

3. Take a few seconds to review the Pays.

Single-line machines always have the payouts posted on the front of the machine either at the top or the bottom of the machine.

Video machines however will have a SEE PAYS button or RULES button on the screen or on the front of the machine. Press this button and then scroll your way through the pages (by pressing NEXT) to see what the pays are and what you need for the Bonus game. Read carefully the instructions for the Bonus game so you won't have to ask the person beside you what you need to do when you get the Bonus.

You should also make a point of checking if the payouts have been changed from the last time you played your favorite machine. I have noticed that a lot of the payouts, particularly on machines in Las Vegas, are being changed so that they are less favorable to the slot player.

Check out the example above on a favorite game of mine – CHOY SUN DOA.

When I play this REEL Machine these are the normal payouts I get. Please note that in a REEL machine the payouts are independent of the number of reels played. In other words regardless of the number of reels played you will always get the payout indicated by the pay line if the symbol appears in the middle of the reels you are not playing. For example, if you get 5 dragons on the screen in the middle line you will get 800 credits regardless of the number of reels you play since the dragons are all on the middle line and therefore count towards the payout. This is an important attribute of this type of game. This is the reason I can play three reels and still get five of a kind as long as the last two symbols of the five of a kind are in the middle of the fourth and fifth reels. You would be amazed at how often this happens.

The first thing you should notice about this machine is what the payouts are for three of a kind. Since this is by far the most frequent payout you will get it makes some sense that you should structure your bet so you can at least recover the amount you bet on each spin otherwise your money will not last very long. The first thing we notice is that 5 credits is the least amount you can win (paid out for three 9's or three 10's). This is not very promising since the only way you can cover this bet is to play two reels for three credits and hope the third symbol lands in the middle of the third reel. This is not a good idea. My preference is to try to find a bet that will payout on the first three reels and will cover my bet most of the time. To do this I will bet three reels (7 credits) with an 8 times multiplier. Consequently I will win 40 credits if I get three 9"s or 10"s thereby losing 16 (7 x 8 = 56 – 40) credits. But for any other three-symbol win I will more than cover my bet. You can play much longer when the machine returns more than you bet than you can when you are losing money even when you get a win.

Now look at what they have done in Las Vegas to encourage us to play more lines. In the example below (for the same CHOY SUN DOA game) they have changed the payouts based on the number of reels you play.

		REEL 1	REEL 1-2	REEL 1-3	REEL 1-4	REEL 1-5		
	5	300	300	300	500	800	5	
	4	50	50	50	50	50	4	
	3	20	20	20	20	20	3	
	5	300	300	300	500	800	5	
	4	35	35	35	35	35	4	
	3	15	15	15	15	15	3	
	5	200	200	200	200	200	5	
	4	30	30	30	30	30	4	
	3	10	10	10	10	10	3	
	5	200	200	200	200	200	5	
	4	20	20	20	20	20	4	
	3	10	10	10	10	10	3	

ALL WINS SHOWN WITH 1 CREDIT BET. ALL WINS SHOWN IN CREDITS.
ALL WINS BEGIN WITH LEFTMOST REEL AND PAY LEFT TO RIGHT ONLY ON ADJACENT REELS.

1¢ Buys
1 Credit

To see this more clearly let's assume that you are playing my favorite bet – three reels and an 8 times multiplier for 56 credits. In the original payout (above) you would receive 300 credits for 5 fish. If the fish on reels 4 and 5 were located on the middle line then this payout would be worth 2400 credits (300 x 8).

In the newer payout table (above) you would still get the same 2400 credits because you are playing 3 reels. However, if you were playing 5 reels you would get a 6400-credit payout. In this way the casino is trying to entice you to play more reels. Don't be fooled however, you are still better to bet fewer reels but a bigger multiplier. In the long run you will play longer and win bigger.

5.4 Determining How Many Lines to Play

If you are playing a Progressive slot machine you really have no choice but to play the maximum number of credits (maximum number of lines and the maximum multiplier) to qualify for the jackpot prize. I usually play these machines only when I am up money. You are always better to play these machines with the casino's money and not your own.

However, if you are not playing a Progressive slot machine then there are a number of decisions to make.

On a single line machine the amount to spend is usually quite simple since there is only one factor – the multiplier. You have probably heard by now that the payout percentage on a dollar machine is better than on a nickel machine and a nickel machine payout percentage is better than a penny machine. While this was true when penny machines first appeared this is no longer the case. What is true is that there are more stops on a Virtual slot machine than there are on a modern Mechanical slot machine therefore the frequency of getting a win on a Mechanical slot machine (with a fixed drum) is always better than on a Virtual slot machine with many more stops. This doesn't stop people from betting more on a penny machine – given that there are more lines and multipliers than there are typically on dollar machines. In fact in most casinos penny slots greatly out number dollar slots. This wasn't the case just a few years ago.

The following table shows typical lines and multipliers for most slot machines:

Denominations	Lines	Multipliers	Max. Bet
Dollar	1, 3, 5	1, 2, 3	$15.00
Quarter	1, 3, 5	1, 2, 3	$3.75
Nickel	1, 2, 3, 5, 9	1, 2, 3, 4, 5	$2.25
Penny	1, 5, 10, 15, 20	1, 2, 5, 10, 20	$4.00

What you need to ask yourself is would you play $3 or more on a dollar slot machine. If the answer is yes then the amount you will play on a slot machine is probably not an issue so go ahead and bet the maximum and skip to the end of the book because there is nothing more I can say to influence your play and help you get more for your entertainment dollar.

However, if your answer is no and you would never play $3 or more on a dollar slot machine then why are you betting the maximum on a quarter, nickel or penny slot machine?

The probability of hitting a jackpot on any slot machine is very low. It is so low in fact that there is no significant difference in hitting it on 1 pay line or the maximum number of pay lines. This is particularly true of the modern Video slot machine that could have a large number of stops on each virtual reel. It's like being struck by lightening once or twice. In both cases the probability of either event happening to you is extremely low.

An example might help to explain how this works in practice. Let's use the simple slot machine I built in *Section 2.3 EPROMs and Random Number Generators*. You may remember (if you didn't skip this section) that there were 32,768 possible outcomes on this very simple machine. Twelve of these outcomes would result in a jackpot meaning that the chance of getting a jackpot on this machine is 0.0003662 (12/32,768). In other words it is very small. Let's also remember that this is a simple example and on a real slot machine where there may be hundreds of virtual stops (not 32 as in our simple example) the chance of winning a jackpot is even smaller. So what's the point of this – well if the chance of winning a jackpot is really small then whether you play 9 lines or 20 lines the chance of winning in either case will still be really small. In fact there are people who only play 1 pay line. However, I do not recommend this approach.

My preference is to play 9 pay lines or in the event there are not 9 pay lines then the nearest number of lines to 9. If the machine only has 9 pay lines (like a lot of nickel machines) I will then bet 5 pay lines. Remember never to play the maximum number of lines. You will loose your money too quickly and you will not significantly increase you chance of winning.

I call this the **Nines Rule**.

This technique works because payouts usually occur from the left-hand side of the screen to the right-hand side. This means that in order to get any payout you are most likely to cross one of the first 9 pay lines. If you still need convincing, take a look at the payouts for each pay-line on any slot machine. These are the graphs that you see at the end of the game rules. The percentage of winning lines after the ninth pay-line drop-off significantly. Any time you play more than 9 pay-lines you are just throwing your money away. This doesn't mean that you will never win on a higher pay line than 9 (of course you will and people do every day), it just means that the chance of this happening isn't worth the risk of betting more than 9 lines.

5.5 Deciding the Multiplier to Play

Once you've decided on the number of lines to play, the next decision is the multiplier to play. As I said earlier there are a lot of players who will play the maximum number of lines but will only bet a 1 times multiplier. They probably do this to keep the total cost down. However, this is not a good way to play since a single multiplier often doesn't even return enough to cover your bet. Think of the number of times you have played 40 credits (in the case of the DAVINCI DIAMONDS machine above that would be 20 lines with a 2 times multiplier – I see people play this way all the time) only to be returned 20 credits (10 times 2) for the smallest three symbol win. It is hard to play for very long if you are betting 40 credits and only getting 20 credits back.

A better strategy is to play 9 pay lines with a 5 times multiplier for 45 credits and be returned 50 credits instead of 20 credits for the same win. This will at least cover your bet and allow you to play a little longer.

For example, when I play Texas Tea I always bet 5 pay lines (since 9 is the maximum number of lines) with a 5 times multiplier (25 credits) instead of playing 9 pay lines with a 5 times multiplier (45 credits). Every time I get a win I get the same amount as playing the maximum bet but I only put a little more than ½ the amount at risk.

Similarly, when I play a REEL machine, like the POMPEII example below, I usually play 3 reels (9 credits in this example) with an 8x multiplier for a total bet of 72 credits but on this machine the multipliers were higher so I elected to play only a 5x multiplier for a total bet of 45 credits. This is considerably less than the maximum bet of 5 reels (25 credits) with the maximum multiplier (10 times) or 250 credits. I get over 5 times the playtime and still have a good chance of winning a substantial amount.

In the POMPEII example above you win 200 credits for getting 5Ks (the volcanoes are wild). If you were to play 5 reels for 25 credits with a 2x multiplier or 50 credits in total (like a lot of people do) you would only have won 8,000 credits for getting 5Ks (200 x 2 x 15 = 6,000) and another 5Ks (200 x 2 x 5 = 2,000) for your 50-credit bet. However, if you played 3 reels (9 credits) with a 5x multiplier for a total of 45 credits (as I did) you would have won 20,000 credits or 2.5 times the payout of the person who played 5 credits more.

I was explaining this strategy to my wife once on a POMPEII machine (she usually played 5 reels with a 1 times multiplier because she didn't want to wager more than 25 credits). I suggested she play 3 reels (7 credits) with a 3 times multiplier for a total of 21 credits. This was less than her usual bet but once she started to do this she found she actually made more money while putting less money at risk.

I almost always bet the <u>Maximum Multiplier</u>. One exception to this rule is when the multipliers are very large. In some Las Vegas casinos we now see REEL machines with 10 and 20 times multipliers. They also increase the bet per reel (as in the example above) so a three-reel bet like the one in the example below now costs 9 credits to play instead of 7 credits. I don't usually play these machines (I usually look for the one that costs 7 credits to play 3 reels) but I did so on this occasion because I had just won on the machine above and, as you can see I got a nice $200 payout for my 90-cent bet.

If you are betting the maximum number of lines and the maximum multiplier every time you play then try this technique instead. You will have just as much fun, your money will last a lot longer and in the long run because you will get more spins you might actually win more money.

If you do not usually bet the maximum number of lines and the maximum multiplier then experiment by picking a number of lines and a multiplier that you are comfortable with but puts a smaller amount at risk. <u>Pick a multiplier that will at least pay you your total bet back on a small (three-symbol) win</u>. Three-symbol wins are the most common so if you can cover your bet on one of these you will always make money on a four or five-symbol win. In the example above POMPEII also pays on a two-symbol 9 or 10. The machine will pay 5 credits on these two wins times the multiplier. When you play an 8 times multiplier you will win 40 (5 x 8) credits. This means you will lose 16 credits on a 56-credit bet but this is still a lot better than losing 40 credits on a 50-credit (25 x 2) bet because you only win 10 credits with a 2 times multiplier.

I call this the **Cover My Bet (CMB) Rule**. So always play a combination of number of lines and a multiplier that will payout more than your bet on a three symbol win (since these are the wins you get most frequently). If you play a REEL Machine always play at least 3 reels because most wins are 3-symbols and by playing 3 reels you will always get paid for every 3 symbol win. This is not always true for a line machine where the 3 symbols may be on a line you are not playing.

Although my favorite bet is the 56-credit bet, I will randomly make a 75-credit bet (playing 4 reels for 15 credits with a 5 times multiplier) when I am playing. I will seldom bet more than 100 credits. In the example below I bet 75 credits and won the bonus game. During the bonus game I got this win for 56,250 credits. It is worth mentioning, that if I had got this win during my 56-credit bet I would have won 67,200 credits. However you can not think of it this way because if I had continued with my 56-credit bet I might not have got the bonus game at all and therefore not had this win in any case. In the same way you have to start blocking out the near misses because, as I said earlier, near-misses are programmed to occur 30 % of the time so even if you had been playing more lines or reels you would not have got the win.

5.6 How Long to Stay at a Machine

There is nothing worse than sitting at a slot machine and watching your money disappear quickly. Not having any payouts, just the sound of the spin button being pushed or the handle pulled and the reels turning.

This is the very reason that I use the following technique every time I sit down at a new machine. I call this the **Loose Slot Test (LST) Technique**:

1. First, as I described above, I decide how many credits I plan to play (the number of lines times the multiplier).

2. I then play 10 spins (you might pick another number but I like to use 10 spins).

3. I then multiply the number of credits I plan to play by the number of spins to determine the total amount I will invest in the machine before moving on. For example, if I am playing a POMPEII machine and I decide to play 56 credits per spin and 10 spins in total then the total amount I am putting at risk is 560 credits.

4. I then count off ten spins.

5. After the 10th spin I should have 560 credits less than what I started with if I did not win any payouts. For example, if I started with 2,000 credits then after ten spins with no payouts I should have 1,440 credits left (2,000 – 560 = 1,440).

6. I then take the difference between the number of credits I actually have in the machine, given that I actually did win a few payouts and 1,440 credits to determine the amount I actually did win.

7. I divide this number by 56 to determine how many pulls I still have left. For example, let's assume I did win something on my 10 spins and I now have 1,780 credits in the machine. This means I still have 370 (1,780 – 1,440) credits or 6 (340/56 ~ 6) spins left.

8. I then count off 6 spins and repeat steps 5 and 6. As soon as my credits fall to 1,440 or less I cash out and leave the machine.

9. If however, I get above the original 2,000 credits I started with then I continue in the same way except I will now have more than the 10 spins I started with. For example, let's suppose I have 2,450 credits after my first 10 spins. This means I still have 1,010 (2,450 − 1,440) credits or 18 (1,010/56 ~ 18) spins left. I then repeat step 8 above by counting off the 18 spins. If you are lucky enough to have found a Loose Slot Machine and continue to win at it, then use the Box Technique described in the next section to make sure you retain some of your winnings.

An alternative way to perform this test is to play with a small denomination bill (say $5) and either play until you lose it or you start to win. Both techniques will work.

I prefer the former because it forces me to think about what I'm doing and the rate at which the trend is moving. I also hate to get to the end of my test and have only enough money left for a partial play. If I have more money remaining than I need I can at least make a full play on the last spin. There is nothing worse than playing 1 credit as your last pull and winning the Bonus game. I can't tell you how many times this has happened to me. So make one last pull with the total amount you have been playing and then leave the machine.

Regardless of whether you count or use a fixed amount to perform the Loose Slot Test it is critical that you move on if you do not get a positive result.

5.7 *What to do When You Have a Winning Machine*

I have seen so many people get a good payout on a machine only to continue to sit at the machine and give it all back.

I have seen more people increase their bets after a payout only to lose their money even more quickly.

I have also seen people get a good payout and then promptly leave the machine. They don't even bother to give it one more pull just to clear the win.

This just reinforces what I already knew – people do not know how to play a winning machine. This is understandable since most slot players do not play winning machines.

Let me share with you my advice on how you can keep more of your winnings when you do find a machine that is actually paying out. The example above is a machine I won on in Bill's Gamblin' Hall and Saloon in Las Vegas. Instead of leaving this machine after the $122 win above, I used the Box Technique described below to continue to play the machine and make an additional $125 before I finally left it. However, before I do so, there is one more important thing you need to know about slot machines.

While every pull results in a random event, there are patterns to every system of random numbers. This may not seem intuitive to you but if you look at a set of randomly generated numbers it is very likely that they will contain a pattern in at least some portion of the numbers if you have a large enough set. I taught statistics part-time at the College level and one of the things I liked to do with the students early in the course was to show them several sets of numbers. A computer randomly generated one set of numbers. I created the other sets. I asked them to try and identify the random set of numbers. They would invariably get it wrong because the random set contained repetitive numbers.

Professor Gregory Chaitin (mathematician and computer scientist) demonstrated this when he showed that you could always prove that there are patterns in every system even a system of randomly generated numbers. Slot players know this instinctively when they get a number of payouts in a short period of time and then go a long time getting nothing from the machine as they wait for the next pattern of favorable outcomes to occur.

Armed with this information and given that you have found a machine that is actually paying something (by this I mean you are getting back more than you are putting into the machine), then I suggest you use the technique described below.

Immediately set yourself a lower and upper limit that you plan to play within. I call this the **Box Technique** (where the top of the box is the upper limit and the bottom of the box is the lower limit). The lower limit is meant to be the number of credits you will stop at and leave the machine. The upper limit is the number of credits at which you will cash out and put the ticket in your pocket or if the machine is still playing you will set new limits.

I usually set these limits as soon as I have <u>tripled</u> the amount I decided to put at risk using the Loose Slot Technique described earlier. By tripling this amount I have some reason to think that I have found a loose machine.

My lower limit is usually <u>twice</u> what I started with and the upper limit is often <u>five times</u> what I started with. For example, if I sit down to play with $20 and using the LST technique described in section *5.6 How Long to Stay at a Machine* I manage to run this up to $60 then I set my limits at $40 and $100. If I drop down to $40 I leave having doubled my money. If I get to $100 then I cash out the ticket and start all over.

Cash out when you are at your upper limit and leave the machine when you go down to your lower limit. This technique requires a lot of discipline but if you have the discipline to follow it you will be surprised at how much longer your money will last. If you follow this technique and use the **GHP** (Going Home Pocket) **Rule** you will be surprised at how much money you will have when you leave the casino.

5.8 Playing Progressive Machines

Playing Progressive machines is not the same as playing other machines.

To start with, a portion of every bet is allocated to the progressive jackpot. The casino usually resets the jackpot at a certain amount once the jackpot is won but the players contribute any amount above the initial amount. In the example above the starting jackpot was $1,000,000. The players contributed everything above that.

The other thing to notice is that you must play the maximum bet to be eligible for the jackpot. In the example above you only win the jackpot if you bet the maximum number of credits (2). If you play 1 credit you only win 2,000 credits not the progressive win. I am amazed at how many people play these machines without putting in the maximum bet. Often they will only play 1 credit. I don't know whether they think the payouts are better on these machines (which they are not) of if they just don't understand that they will not win the jackpot by betting 1 credit.

When I first started playing slot machines I was in Las Vegas with some friends who did not gamble. I carefully explained to one friend who wanted to play progressive video poker that he should bet the maximum to win the jackpot. Everyone then broke up to try his luck. Within 30 minutes a very loud alarm went off and a crowd started to form around the video poker area. My friends and I rushed over to see our friend standing there with a big smile on his face in front of a machine showing a royal flush. The progressive meter read over $1,000,000. We were all delighted but couldn't get near him. Security men surrounded him. After a while they gave him a check and he left the area. When we got to him he showed us the check for $411.25. That's right. He didn't play three coins like I told him, but 1 coin and won the small jackpot prize. He didn't understand what all the fuss was for until we told him again that he could have won over $1,000,000. To this day I'm not sure he really understood what might have been.

You will also note in the example above that the payouts other than the jackpot are relatively small. This is deliberate because people playing these machines are usually only interested in the jackpot and pay little attention to the other wins.

If you play Progressive machines do not use your own money but take any winnings you have and use them. I typically play these machines at the end of my session. I usually set a specific amount I plan to invest, like I would for any machine and leave as soon as I have spent this amount.

6.0 Betting Strategies

In every casino game there is a "house advantage" (sometimes called the house edge). This is the percentage advantage that the house has. Some of the common percentages are: Blackjack – 5.90%, Baccarat – 5.0%, Roulette – 5.26%, and Keno – 20% + depending on the spots picked (1 spot being the smallest house advantage).

With slot machines casinos like to advertise the payout percentage (called payback) as a way of differentiating themselves from other casinos and as a draw to bring in players. After all, the higher the payback the looser the machines – right? The example below is a sign you find outside most casinos in Las Vegas.

In the example above the casino's advantage is only 3% (100% - 97%). In most slot machines the house advantage is usually anywhere from 0.1% (when a very loose machine might payback 99.9%) to 15% (where a very tight machine might only payback 85% - these are usually found at the airport in Las Vegas).

Why the interest in "house advantage"? The simple fact is that whatever casino game you play you will eventually loose all of your money if you play long enough. Guaranteed. Probability Theory proves this. The house advantage over time will eventually relieve you of all of your money. The casinos call this <u>grinding</u>. The house advantage will eventually grind you down if you play long enough and relieve you of all of your cash.

Let's look at an example with the following assumptions:

You start with $100,
You bet $1.00 with each spin,
The machine pays 97% (as above),
You are getting an average return with each spin (which never happens),
You do not take your money out of the machine.

How long would your money last?

You will have nothing left after about 4,500 spins. This may seem like a lot of spins but if you consider how little time it takes to press the spin button, you would probably lose all your money in a couple of hours. If you increased your bet to $5.00 on each spin your money would only last about 30 minutes. This is what grinding means.

My rule of thumb is the dollar a minute test. Twenty dollars will last an average player about 20 minutes in a casino playing slot machines. If you do better than this you are ahead of the game. The next time you go into a casino with $100 see if you can beat Mike's dollar test and last 2 hours.

The only chance you have to try and gain an edge is to have a sound betting strategy. This is very evident in table games but can also be carried over to slot play. A betting strategy will not stop you from losing all your money if you play long enough but it will allow you to play longer and get more value out of your entertainment dollar.

The betting strategy I prefer to use for slot machines is simpler than what I use for table games but it is effective. The strategy is based on betting more when you are winning and less when you are losing. I call this the **Snakes & Ladders Strategy**. Of course this strategy only applies when you have decided to stay at a machine for an extended play. Otherwise you would just follow the guidelines I laid out in section *5.6 How Long to Stay at a Machine*.

This strategy also only applies to players who are <u>not</u> betting the maximum multiplier. If you are betting the maximum multiplier then your betting strategy is implicit using the technique I described in section *5.5 Deciding the Multiplier to Play*. However, if you are not playing the maximum multiplier you need an edge and this is where the betting strategy comes in.

If you win you are on a **Ladder** and you increase your bet, if you lose you are on a **Snake** so you decrease your bet. Using this simple betting strategy you can extend your play.

Let's assume that your preferred bet is 10 lines (less than the maximum of 25 lines) and your multiplier is 3x (less than the maximum of 5x). The number of lines to play was determined by you per section *5.4 Determining How Many Lines to Play*. In this strategy you are <u>not</u> going to change the number of lines you play – in this example you will always play 10 lines. The strategy therefore, is as follows:

1. Always bet your preferred multiplier (in the above example this would be 3x) when you first sit down at the machine.

2. Continue to bet this multiplier until you have won nothing in three consecutive spins.

3. Drop down one multiplier from your preferred multiplier (in this example you would drop down to 2x).

4. Continue to bet this multiplier until you have won nothing in three consecutive spins. If you do win more than your bet on any one spin then repeat the strategy from step 1.

5. If you have not won more than you bet in the three consecutive spins above, drop down one more multiplier (in this example 1x).

6. Continue to bet this multiplier until you win more than your bet on any one spin then go to step 1 and repeat the cycle.

7.0 Closing Remarks

As I said at the outset there is no way to beat a slot machine. The probability of you actually winning a large jackpot is probably worse than being struck by lightening – twice. The very best you can do is to extend your play and get more value for your entertainment dollar. If you follow my guidelines and tips you will go home more often with money – not necessarily more money than you brought to the casino but some money and just as important you will have had some great entertainment.

If you enjoyed the book and if it was of some help to you, maybe provided some entertainment value, helped you play longer at the casino or just made it easier for you to take some money home please take a moment to write a review on Amazon. Reviews are important to an Author because in many cases they are the only feedback we get. They can also be invaluable to others, like you, who are looking for a *Guide to Better Slot Play*.

Cross-Reference

I have added these cross-references to trap the most important ideas in *Mike's Guide to Better Slot Play* so you will have one place to go to refresh your memory of what was said and to provide a reference to the location in the text where the idea is fleshed out. There is nothing worse than looking for something in the text and knowing it is there but not being able to find it.

Each point is prefixed with its location in *Mike's Guide to Better Slot Play*.

p. 1 - **Mike's Golden Rule**: Before going to the casino, decide how much cash you will take with you (never more than you can afford), set a time limit on how long you will play and never bring a credit card or bankcard into the casino. Leave the casino immediately when you are out of money or out of time.

p. 9 - All modern slot machines are controlled by a computer chip (**EPROM**) programmed with a Random Number Generator (**RNG**) that is running constantly in the machine. The results of a spin are determined immediately when the spin button is pressed or the handle pulled. The spin of the reels has nothing to do with the result. The spinning reels are only there to provide entertainment value.

p. 13 - The manufacturers program slot machines to payout at a predetermined percentage.

p. 15 - There are four kinds of slot machines: modern **Mechanical** slot machines, **Video** slot machines, **REEL** slot machines and **Progressive** slot machines.

p. 24 - In setting up the virtual stops on a modern slot machine the manufacturer has created a number of "**near misses**" (about 30% of the results are near misses).

p. 24   - The best paying slot machines in order of decreasing performance are: a) modern Mechanical machines; b) REEL machines; c) Video machines and d) Progressive machines.

p. 25   - Common slot machine **myths**: always make the maximum bet; leave the machine as soon as you win big; this machine is going to pay off if I just play it a little longer; I left a machine and the next person to play it won a jackpot that should have been mine; the casino is tightening its slots; machines at the entrance and end of aisles pay better. All of these statements are false.

p. 29   - Make sure you have a **Going Home Pocket** somewhere separate from the rest of your money where you can put the money you have won to take it home with you. Do not use this money to gamble with.

p. 37   **Loose slot machines** can be found; on elevated carousels, near crossovers, near cafes, snack bars, change booths and ATMs.

p. 37   - **Tight slot machines** are located: in secluded areas; casino entrances; near ticket and show lines; surrounding the table games and near sports books. Never play slot machines at the airport in Las Vegas.

p. 40   - If you have a choice of machines to play, play the one with the largest win meter (winner paid window). I call this the **Pay & Pay Again Rule.**

p. 41   - **Always check the rules** before you play a machine that's new to you. Review the Pays, Bonus Game rules (if any), the number of lines available to you and the multiplier before you start to play.

p. 52   - Use the **Nines Rule** to determine the number of lines to play. Play the nearest integer number of lines to 9 available on the machine. If there are 9 lines maximum then play 5 lines. Never play the maximum number of lines.

p. 57   - **Always play the maximum multiplier**. If this is too expensive for you use the **CMB Rule** (Cover My Bet) and pick a multiplier such that a three-symbol payout will return you at least the amount bet.

p. 59   - Use the **LST Technique** to find a loose slot machine. Start by playing 10 spins. Count how many credits you have won after ten spins. Divide that by the number of credits you are playing per spin and play that number of spins. Repeat the process until you have no spins left in which case you should move on to another machine. If you have won more than the credits for 10 spins then use the Box Technique to increase your winnings.

p. 62   - Use the **Box Technique** to extend your winnings when you are on a winning machine. Set yourself upper and lower limits to play within. If you win more than your upper limit then reset the limits and continue on. When you fall below the lower limit stop playing, put the money you have won in your Going Home Pocket and leave the machine.

p. 64   - **Progressive Machines** – always bet the maximum number of credits.   Play these machines only when you have winnings and set a specific limit on how much you will play with.

p. 68   - Betting Strategies only apply to players who are <u>not</u> betting the maximum multiplier. Use the six step **Snakes & Ladders Strategy** by increasing and decreasing the multiplier based on winning more than your total bet during three consecutive spins.

About the Author

M. J. Veaudry holds a Bachelor Degree In Computer Science and a Masters Degree in Business Administration. He has held a number of senior management positions in the computer industry and was a partner with one of the world's largest professional services firms. As a management consultant he has worked in Asia, Canada and the US.

As a gaming aficionado he has had a long-time interest in playing and betting strategies as they relate to Las Vegas table games and slot machines.

If you enjoyed *Mike's Guide to Better Slot Play* you might also enjoy reading one of Mike's other books (also available in paperback and electronic form)

Mike's Guide to Las Vegas is a travel guide with emphasis on Las Vegas table games, including Mike's favorites: Blackjack, Pai Gow Poker, Roulette, Craps and Let It Ride. The book will explain these popular table games in simple to understand language with betting strategies and a step-by-step process to get you to the table so you can play with confidence.

What some readers have said about *Mike's Guide to Las Vegas*:

"I enjoyed the straight forward approach with a friendly touch of humor. … Reading this guide feels like you are having a conversation with Mike as he addresses your questions just as they pop up."
– Carolyn Stewart

"This guide saves a great deal of time - especially if you only go to Vegas every couple of years or so. Thanks Mike for making our trip a great one…"
– H. Cameron

"We used Mike's Guide to Las Vegas every day of our trip! It was filled with both fun and practical information and made getting around very simple… Thanks Mike for a great book and helping to make our trip a lot better."
– Paul Croisier

FRAUD - Don't Be A Victim takes a look at personal frauds in several common venues: credit cards, debit cards, telephones, email, Internet, identity and public areas. The book will describe typical scams in each of these areas and focus on ways to identify them and protect you from being duped. Seniors are a large target group for fraudsters and the book pays special attention to protecting this large and vulnerable group.

1471440R00044

Made in the USA
San Bernardino, CA
20 December 2012